T0114745

Buried in the
Debris of Independence

Copyright 2020 T.S.E. Katsulukuta

All rights reserved. No part of this publication may be reproduced, stored in a retrieval system, or transmitted in any from or by any means, electronic, mechanical, photocopying, recording or otherwise without prior permission from the publishers.

Published by
Luviri Press
P/Bag 201 Luwinga
Mzuzu 2

ISBN   978-99960-66-50-4
eISBN 978-99960-66-51-1

The Luviri Press is represented outside Africa by:
African Books Collective Oxford (order@africanbookscollective.com)

www.luviripress.blogspot.com
www.africanbookscollective.com

Buried in the Debris of Independence

The Life and Death of Rev Alexander Kutchona

T.S.E. Katsulukuta

Biographies of People and Parishes no. 2

Luviri Press
Mzuzu
2020

Acknowledgements

I am greatly indebted to many people including daughters to late Reverend Kutchona Mbewe who were more than willing to share with me whatever they could remember about their father.

Reverend Dr van Deventer, Prof Martin Pauw and my wife Phyllis and children and many others who read through the manuscript and gave suggestions and encouragement. Reverend Leonard Katundu also played an important part in the later stages of the book.

I also thank Mr Mkanda who did the initial typing.

However, people who played their part in the production of this booklet are too numerous to be mentioned by name; they all deserve to be thanked.

Table of Contents

Introduction

We came to a forest of thickly interwoven *mkandankhuku* hedges. Waving his right hand over the hedges, one of my two escorts said to me, "Rev Kutchona's grave is somewhere in this direction." I sighed to myself. Another barrier? The bushes were very thick above the hips, but they were less dense at the bottom. For seventy yards we crawled on our knees. Then we saw two whitewashed tombs. My escorts looked at me again saying, "Rev Kutchona's grave is to the north and Olafi's is to the south."

On hearing this, I quickened my steps past them in order to get a clear view of the inscription on the graves. The bush had been cleared one yard around the tombs, and so I went around them twice. But there was nothing written on them. Disappointed I sighed again. "Mystery!"

Thirty or forty yards away to the east, the grave of Kutchona's wife, Ester, stood conspicuous on a well-cleared ground. The inscription clearly reads: Ester Kutchona Thyolamanja. Born 1907 - Died 29.12.97 - Buried 31.12.97. This grave was constructed just two years after her death. Rev Kutchona's grave had been forgotten and left unattended from 1964 to 1999, the time relatives constructed a tombstone over Ester's grave.

Rev Kutchona died in the immediate aftermath of Malawi's Independence and it shows that the movement was dynamite. In the debris of the Independence explosion Kutchona himself was buried, his brilliant life and ministry were overshadowed by thick dust arising from the collapse of the white man's rule. The years immediately before and after independence were characterized by brutal and mysterious murders of innocent citizens. Everybody lived in terror instead of the peace that our leaders proclaimed in the party slogan at the beginning of every meeting. For forty years the martyr has been consciously buried

6

in the sub-consciousness of the Malawian society and the people deliberately lived as if it had never happened. A mere mention of his name was bothersome to the conscience of Malawi.

His wife Ester, his children and relatives were greatly affected by his death. They lived in perpetual fear and untold suffering, since Malawi dealt with their father as the country had done with many others listed in their "traitors' books." But Ester and the children had to go on living despite the tragedy. They had to try to exist in the same ruthless country whose independence cost their father's life and whose citizenry was so indifferent to his brutal murder. What other better way was there for them to forge ahead, rather than to try and forget and erase him from their memories! Consequently, they did not keep much of the record of those tragic events.

Rev Kutchona, being a church minister of Nkhoma Synod of the Church of Central Africa Presbyterian, the office of the General Secretary demanded an explanation from the Government on the brutal murder of their outspoken minister of God's word. The Government responded with a sense of indifference and refused to say anything on the matter.[1] Unfortunately, this correspondence could not be found in the archives, where they were kept. (The mysterious disappearance of revealing documents was not strange.)

Kutchona Mbewe's death story was not even featured in *Kuunika*, the official magazine of Nkhoma Synod. The church seemed alarmed by the Government's attitude of indifference on this incident. Besides, the headquarters of the Synod was attacked by swarming youth leaguers disguised in 'Nyau' masks. The General Secretary himself escaped murder attempts several times. The church was silenced and she

---

[1] Information from Rev Killion Mgawi, then General Secretary.

decided to pursue the issue no further, and Rev Kutchona was deleted from her memory as well.

Chapter 1

A Brilliant Pupil Turns into a Diligent Teacher

Alexander Kutchona's father was Mazoni, a reputed teacher from the Kachere family. Kachere was a Chief among the Ngoni immigrants who had come into the country from South Africa through the Domwe hills, settling at Maonde, Dedza. Mazoni had eight boys and one girl. His firstborn son was Alexander and two of Alexander's brothers were Dinkan and Lester.

These people had long encountered the whites in South Africa and they easily associated with the white missionaries who had also come from South Africa and settled in the Central Region.

Land at Maonde was not big enough for these new settlers and Kachere sent his son Richard (brother of Pemba) to look for land at Chikoma where they would settle. Richard took with him a good number of immigrant families and they founded a village near Katewe, named after their leader, Richard.

"As a boy, he intently learned the skills of using shield and spear in war. He listened diligently as the elders narrated to the young ones how they conquered the indigenous people as they came all the way from South Africa. It is possible that Alexander himself had witnessed some of these raids here in Malawi, for he later told of them with moving details," said Chikakuda, a distant cousin of Kutchona.[2]

As a son of a teacher, Alexander also aspired to become a teacher like his father. He was brilliant and always attentive in class. Mr Kutchona, teacher and father, was very proud of this serious student. Among the

---

[2] S.E. Chikakuda, Dedza, 5.5.2003.

sons of Mazoni, Alexander excelled and completed all school grades of that time to become a teacher of Vernacular grade like his father. The missionaries gave him more learning until he acquired Teaching grade status. Among the early schools where he taught was Kalulu School at Richard village.

He betrothed Ester Thyolamanja; Nabetha was her clan name. She was a daughter to a very reputable teacher around Chikoma. The girl was short and stout and had a short face as well. She was light in complexion and appeared thoughtful and yet always welcoming. Ester was shy and her voice was calm, but she was firm and confident in her speech.

Kutchona was tall and slim, but his body was firm and strong like a *naphini* tree. He had a long face and was dark in complexion. He had a loose tongue and he seldom paused to think when he was talked to.

What a contrast of personalities! And what could have brought them together? Could it be their common love for singing? Was it through family arrangements? I mean, did the teacher parents, who were already related, arrange the marriage for Alexander and Ester, as was the prevailing custom of the time? Or should we speculate that it was a teacher/pupil relationship? Their courting still remains a mystery, but their wedding was not. One day Alexander and Ester walked all the way to Mphunzi Mission. On that beautiful day the couple stood in wedlock before Reverend Bwana Rens, I suppose, and it was one of the first weddings at this mission station. It certainly was the first Christian wedding in the Katewe/Chikoma area. Alexander was four years older than Ester but both of them were relatively young when they married.

Ester soon became expectant and gave birth to a baby boy, presumably in 1923. But this child died the same year he was born. She conceived again and Alefina was born in 1924. She was a great consolation to the young couple who had started parenthood tragically. The death of their

10

first child had caused them so much pain that they desired to forget it. Hence they always talked of Alefina as being their first born.

Alefina was peerless and the parents quickly noted her want of company. One night Ester discussed it with Alexander and he suggested that she should approach her younger sister, who had a son slightly older than Alefina. When the two sisters talked it over, Ester took her sister's son, Letison Kalambalala, into her home. Ester and Alexander lived with Letison as if he was one of their own sons. Most people did not notice that Letison was an adopted son to Alexander and Ester.

After Letison, Alexander and Ester adopted more children from relatives. They had a special gift in that. One of those children was Anderson Kutchona, son of Lesten, Alexander's younger brother. One day when Alexander visited Maonde he was greatly concerned to learn that Lesten did not send Anderson to school. Alexander took him and immediately registered him in school. He paid for him up to Junior Certificate level. After passing JC, he successfully went through a Medical Assistants' course. And when the political wind blew, he flew with it to become shadow MP for Dedza west. Tragically he was alleged to have associated himself with the people who later plotted Alexander's murder.

The children born to Alexander and Ester were five daughters and four sons: Lucas came after Alefina. Two girls, Kaleni and Ikesi successively came after him. Taneki came after Ikesi. Binaya and Asibu followed. Naomi, who later changed her name to Dorothy, tailed Asibu, and Olafi was their last born. Some of them are not common names, and Naomi commented, "I do not know where my father got these names from."

Chonde is one of the schools where Alexander taught when he was still youthful and energetic. He taught there from 1934 to 1939. From Chonde, Kutchona went to Maonde. One of his brilliant students there was late Rev Chinkhadze, who described his teacher as "diligent, dedicated, a teacher who knew how to teach well." Chinkhadze also remembered his teacher as being strict, but of good heart. It was Kutchona who recommended Chinkhadze for a teaching course at Mphunzi Mission Station.

He made an impression on his pupils with his love for the Scriptures, for prayer and singing. When late Chinkhadze mentioned singing, he immediately broke into singing the two most favourite songs of his teacher, which he often sang in class:

'Far, far away ... who will go salvation story telling...' and the Chichewa song, 'Pakusenza mtanda.'

For Kutchona, the teaching profession reached its zenith with his stay at Maonde and he later received the calling to serve God as a Church Minister. After a few years at Maonde, the Education Committee of the Presbytery of Nkhoma chose him and two others to be supervisors of schools, among many teachers in the Central Region where the Presbytery operated. The three underwent a supervisors' course at Nkhoma. Kutchona came back to Maonde after the course and he continued residing there as he discharged his duties as supervisor of schools.

The "Mgulupa," as the supervisor of schools was locally called, was also overseer of Sunday school and catechumen classes, working under and in collaboration with a Church Minister. Alexander Kutchona worked under Rev Kachingwe, and this was another contrast of personalities. Kachingwe was slightly taller and he stood with a slight stoop. He appeared to be solemn, but always brightened up into cheers whenever he met people. His face was much lighter in complexion and he responded to people calmly and with courtesy. Kutchona didn't mind much about courtesy and said things straightforward, as long as he believed he was stating the truth, whether it would hurt or not.

Surprisingly the two collaborated very well in their service and they used to confide in each other. Very often Kachingwe entrusted parish work to Kutchona. Most of the time they were seen working together on the church programmes. They were also seen chatting together most of the days. Late Chizinga remarked on the relationship of Kutchona and Kachingwe "I believe Kutchona's calling to the Holy Ministry fermented during those years he lived with Kachingwe and the latter's life influenced his calling a great deal."

But Rev Chinkhadze recalled that pupils had always singled him out as a sure candidate for the ministry. In fact, everyone knew that sooner or later Kutchona would quit teaching to become a full time preacher.

Chapter 2

Kutchona's Calling and Ministry

A steadily glowing fire inside his heart must have burdened his soul for a long time. He wrestled day and night with the question: How would he become a minister of God's word?

Prevailing procedure in Nkhoma Presbytery at that time was that candidates for theological college were picked by the Presbytery officials from evangelists (*alaliki*) who had been long serving teachers. Kutchona was just one of many young qualified teachers, though he had the advantage of being a supervisor. He would have to wait for his turn to be chosen and by then he could even be around sixty or seventy. Yet, the call was already too hot to keep. He struggled with the question: Is this calling ever going to materialize?

I guess he discussed it frequently with Rev Kachingwe as they were chatting on the veranda of the latter's manse. I cannot speculate how the latter responded to his inquisitive young friend. But the real answer would soon come from God.

Procedure for taking candidates for theological training was revisited in the Presbytery meeting of 1943. The meeting decided that the presbytery would no longer hand pick prospective trainees from the evangelists, but candidates to the Theological College would first apply to the Presbytery, before being shortlisted and interviewed. Only those who succeeded in the interview would be accepted for the Theological Training.

This was the first thing that Kachingwe reported to Kutchona when he came from the meeting, and Kutchona wrote his application letter the same day. A few days later he cycled to Nkhoma to deliver the letter by

14

hand. He was on the list of people shortlisted for the interviews. After the interview, Kutchona nearly danced when he learnt that he had been taken for the Theological Course.

The last group of hand-picked students was in college from 1942 to 1944. According to Rev Chinkhadze, a group of ten people recruited through interviews came into the college the same year 1944. *Mthenga*, the newsletter of the Presbytery, which later changed to the current *Kuunika* Magazine, gives nine names of Kutchona's class as follows:[3] Amos Dembo Mvula, Killion Kalumo Banda, Fredrick Chikapa, Jeliel Mphako Phiri, Peter Chamwanza Phiri, Jameson Kuseni Lungu, Josaphat Steven Mwale, Alexander Kutchona Mbewe and his home boy, Stephen Tandani Chanza. All of them were great thinkers, men of deep faith and outstanding personalities. Most of them had excelled in their teaching profession before they came to the Theological College. Kutchona had the additional characteristic of being the most outspoken of the group.

Nkhoma Theological College had the motto "Arise and Shine" (*Nyamuka Wala*). It had two missionary tutors, Revs J.W. Minnaar and J.T.D. Stegmann, two great men of God. Minnaar was addicted to tobacco; he even smoked in class. However, he was Spirit-filled. Late Mataka challenged preachers who propagated that smokers will go to hell, saying, "who of these preachers can compare to Minnaar in holiness?" The puritan, late Rev. J.S. Mwale described the two tutors as men who were "full of prayer and Christ's love."[4] These two men

---

[3]   *Kuunika*, 1947, no. 5, Vol. 29.

[4]   Jonathan Kamwana, "The Spirituality of Rev. J.S. Mwale," DTh, Stellenbosch University, 1997," p. 42.

15

groomed Kutchona at the theological college. They made a mark on the lives of the students, including the life of Alexander Kutchona.

Kutchona was jovial and friendly to everyone in his class, but he developed a deeper friendship with J.S. Mwale, K. Kalumo, Peter Chamanza, Fredrick Chikapa and home boy, Stephen Tandani.

Apart from his classmates he joked a lot with Kambirinya, a cousin from Chikoma. The latter was a young man who had been picked by Pretorius to man a mission bookshop. Kutchona frequented the bookshop during his free time. He used to warn his cousin about the latter's desperate hunt for a life partner.

More than once Kutchona caught Kambirinya proposing love to girls from the "Madona Girls Centre." And one day Kutchona said to his cousin, who was standing side by side with a girl from one of the surrounding villages, "Look at this fool. He wants to stay here in this hilly place to join the people who live like monkeys. "The following morning, he followed his cousin to the bookshop, and said to him, "Your head must be full of water. Or is there any grey stuff in there?" He ended up with this advice, " Girls here have manners like monkeys or dogs. But if you want to marry, go home and get a wife from there." Kambirinya went to his home the following weekend. And he proposed love to a girl of Kanyezi who later became his wife.[5]

Time was flying for Kutchona at Nkhoma because the theological training kept him busy with studies during weekdays and practicals on Saturdays and Sundays. Rev J.W. Minnaar encouraged students to start each day with personal devotions at dawn or earlier. And when they came to class, tutors and all students met in the chapel for communal devotions, before they commenced their lessons. The practical activities

---

[5]   Int. E.G. Kambirinya, Kamvuwu, Dowa, 22.4.2003

during the weekend included preaching at the market, visiting the sick at the mission hospital and conducting services in the prayer houses of Nkhoma congregation. Students also went for evangelistic campaigns in the surrounding villages. It was during these moments that the rest of the students came to know Kutchona and Mwale as gifted preachers, well versed in Scripture.

Nine students graduated from Nkhoma Theological College in 1947 carrying with them the banner "Arise and Shine" into nine congregations. *Mthenga* gives their names and date of ordination as follows[6]: Amon Dembo and F. Chikapa on 24th August at Chinthembwe; on 17th September Alexander Kutchona Mbewe and I. Mphako at Mvera and Dzenza; Chamanza Phiri and Kuseni Lungu at Malingunde and Mlanda on the 21st September. After he completed his theological training in 1947, Kutchona was posted to Mvera. Mvera is the first mission station of Nkhoma Presbytery, founded by the first Dutch Reformed Church missionaries: A.C. Murray and T.C.B. Vlok in 1889. During Rev. Kutchona's time the congregation extended to the border with Nkhotakota District and crossed the Lumbadzi river to Balang'ombe sharing borders with Nkhoma.

The place is mostly hilly and it was reportedly overgrown with indigenous trees in those days. My father, who also lived there soon after Kutchona had left, used to tell stories of lions roaming the place even before sunset. But Rev. Kutchona did not feel totally lost. There were Ngoni at Mvera as well. In fact, Chief Chiwere was a Ngoni warrior and there were several Ngoni villages settled among the Chewa of Mvera. Being a mission station, Mvera was also an educational centre. There was a famous Boarding School and white missionaries taught together with their indigenous counterparts. However, they never lived

---

[6] *Mthenga*, 1947, vol 29, Sept-Oct.

in the same area. The black teachers had small houses to the lower West, while the white missionary teachers had big houses on the higher East, well positioned to catch the first rays of the rising sun. Rev. Kutchona was given a house with the black teachers, away from the white missionaries. It was then a rule in mission stations that an indigenous minister should serve under a white missionary. Kutchona served under a youthful minister, Johan Steytler.

Fresh from college, Rev Kutchona visited the flock, from prayer point to prayer point and from house to house, humming his favourite tune "Far, far away…" Mostly he preached from the Old Testament and when he preached, the flock held their necks up and shed tears in response to his messages. After the sermon he would teach them a song or two in Tonic Solfa.

The white missionaries came from an apartheid background. This was reflected in their relationship to the indigenous people. But meanwhile, the spirit to fight against the white domination was growing among the African people. The Nyasaland African Congress represented this in Malawi.

Before the spirit of Africanism, blacks received, without question, whatever the missionaries said. But now they began to oppose whatever the missionaries tried to introduce. Some conflict arose between the missionaries and a group of elders because the whites refused to demolish a house near the manse, which was unoccupied. The whites could not allow a black minister to live in it. Kutchona sided with the white missionaries not to demolish the house. This was not the only time that he collided with the African elders. He came to the rescue of the missionaries very often and some misunderstood him as a man who sought favour from the whites. He had no conflict with the white missionaries during his stay at Mvera.[7] However, this does not mean that he succumbed to all forms of oppression by the white people. Rev Johan Steytler himself experienced him as "a man of few words, but straight as an arrow from a bow ... Not a person to be intimidated. If convinced that something was not in accordance with God's words, he would not hesitate to say so fearlessly."[8]

Meanwhile Rev Tandani, who had been posted to Mlanda mission station, had died after a very brief stay there. Mlanda was another hilly area whose people were mostly Ngoni of Chief Gomani. The presbytery could find no better candidate for this congregation than Alexander Kutchona Mbewe. In 1949 he was posted to Mlanda from Mvera. Rev Labuschagne was the white minister at Mlanda when Kutchona went there. However, the two ministers did not work together long, since Labuschagne went to Mvera on cross transfer with Johan Steytler, Kutchona's former co-worker. Was the transfer a means of preventing conflict between Kutchona and Labuschagne? Did the mission office send Steytler because he had stayed amicably with Kutchona at Mvera?

Ikesi, Kutchona's daughter, well remembers that the two ministers worked together like one person on the church building. Both Alexander and Johan set an example by joining the people in moulding bricks from morning till dark. I wanted to learn from Ikesi: "Of the congregations your father had been serving, which did he enjoy most? She did not hesitate to mention Mlanda as the place. Unfortunately he did not stay long there. The Synod called him to go and serve in the Synod of Harare in Southern Rhodesia in 1953. Zimbabwe was more developed than Nyasaland in terms of infrastructure and economy. It

---

[7]   Rev S. Banda.

[8]   A.S. Labuschagne, *The Missionary*, Fichardtpark: Drufoma Press, 2000, p. 99.

was advantageous for a church minister to be called to serve in that country. However, Kutchona received the call with a mixture of excitement and regret because they would not be allowed to take all their children with them due to the age limit. The couple only took Asibu, Naomi and Olafi with them. They also took one grandchild. They served in Harare Synod for seven years until 1960.

Kutchona served Harare and Gweru congregations while he was in Zimbabwe. From 1953 to 1958 he served Harare congregation and from 1958-1960 he worked in Gweru. Reverend Daneel wrote this in his book *Mbiri ya C.C.A.P. Sinodi ya Harare 1912-1982* about Reverend Kutchona. When Daneel arrived in Zimbabwe, there was no ordained minister in Harare, and he complained at the presbytery meeting, which was held at Kongwe in 1953 August. The presbytery appointed Rev Alexander Kutchona Mbewe and he came to Harare the same year.[9] Alexander Kutchona was remembered for preaching the word of God deeply and, consequently, he drew crowds and the church building at Harare became too small. As a result they extended it in 1954. He was a strong-minded man and he feared no person.[10]

But in Harare congregation he also experienced conflict with a section of the church members. It started as a conflict of interests over a motorbike between himself and an evangelist of the same congregation.

Inus Daneel, a white missionary from South Africa, had bought and offered a motorbike to Rev. Kutchona to assist him in his long travels because the former was impressed with his devotedness to the ministry. But the evangelist argued that *he* was the right person to receive the

---

[9] *Mbiri ya C.C.A.P. Sinodi ya Harare 1912-1982*, p. 25.

[10] Ibid., p. 36.

motorbike because he came to serve in Harare congregation earlier than Rev Kutchona.

At first, it was a conflict between the two of them and the elders. But it soon grew until every parishioner talked about it. The elders soon took sides, too; some were for Rev Kutchona and others were for the Evangelist. The church held several meetings until the final church session resolved the conflict by ruling that the bike should belong to the church.

Rev Kutchona left Harare for Gweru congregation in 1958 and left the motorbike in the custody of Harare congregation. He served God in Gweru until his return to Nyasaland in 1960, where freedom was dawning and the faith of the people was mixed. They believed in their messiah Kamuzu, the Lion of Malawi, on the one hand and in Jesus, the Lion of Judah, on the other hand.

Chapter 3

Sunshine and Thunder in the Home

Rev Alexander Kutchona never showed to anybody that he had problems. Only one person knew his joys and his fears. This one person was Ester, his wife. She was the closest confidant. In this woman shyness, warmth, thoughtfulness and confidence nicely blended together. She was a very wise person and with Alexander they made a wonderful, cheerful and hospitable home. Naomi, commenting on the relationship of her parents, said, "I never saw them quarrel a single day, and I never thought they ever disagreed, until when I was newly married and I had experienced clashes with my late husband. I went to Mum to ask for advice. Mum surprisingly answered; "It's not strange in new marriages. I too experienced the same thing with your father."

Naomi then objected, "Do not cheat me Mum. We never saw him quarrel with you the way our husbands do to us." Ester laughed, "Did you expect us to settle our differences in your presence?"

Ester was almost everything to Alexander; she was also his prayer partner. She used to wake Alexander before dawn and they prayed together every day, more especially in times of difficulty. After their personal devotions, they rang a bell to call the family members to the sitting room. Naomi clearly remembers, "In the morning we gathered just to say a word of prayer together. He never read Scripture and we seldom sang."

The evening gathering was different; it was another lively service of worship. Rev Kutchona loved to sing and he wanted his children to master all the tunes that he knew in the hymn book. The church in his home used to sing six hymns or more before reading Scripture. A sure hymn among the list was hymn 49. ("*E moyo wangawe, utsitsimuketu*")

When it came to singing that hymn, Rev Kutchona sang with full accord. Beside this one, he also loved to sing songs of praise.

Sometimes, when overwhelmed with joy during these devotions, especially when the house congregation had mastered a hymn well, which the church congregation failed to sing, he would spring up excited and shout "Oh, why not! Let's sing this one in the church this coming Sunday for the congregation to learn it. The congregation fails to sing this hymn as well as we have done. This Sunday we will show them that it is not as difficult as they think."

On that particular Sunday, the Minister in his black preaching gown would graciously come down from the pulpit with long strides to join the rest of the family choir, who were already lined up in front of the congregation. Raising his voice above them all, he would walk back to mount the pulpit to continue the service, satisfied.

When it came to Scripture reading during evening devotions, Rev Kutchona was rather selective. He loved passages with messages of encouragement, especially when he was going through trying moments. Kutchona liked the Old Testament and his favourite book was Joshua. The family congregation heard him repeat such passages as Joshua 1:1-9 "Be strong and courageous. Do not tremble or be dismayed, for the Lord your God is with you…" Another passage that he read often is Joshua 24:15 "And if it is disagreeable in your sight to serve the Lord, choose for yourselves today whom you will serve … But as for me and my house, we will serve the Lord."

One other thing that his family members ardently remember about their late father is how he taught them Scripture at home. If some people rated him among serious preachers, his family church experienced him as a funny preacher. He elaborated Scripture with funny stories that sent all house members laughing their lungs out. But in the end, he asked them questions to assess whether they really got the core of the lesson. More often than not, he was disappointed to learn that they had grasped the joke or the story, but they had not gripped the core of the lesson. Then he would lament: "I should stop telling you stories. I do not tell them to you for fun. They are meant to bring home the message."

His relationship with his children was not always sunny. There were times when clouds covered his face and lightening flashed from his eyes, followed by thunder rolls. Giving her view on what she thought of Kutchona as a father, Naomi said, "He was very strict. I should rather say, he was too strict."

Kutchona never allowed his children to go playing with their peers. The only places his daughters could meet playmates were at church and at school. When his children disobeyed he did not hesitate to apply the rod. Unfortunately, despite his strict grip, especially on the girls, trage-dies still happened. One such incident, as the late Rev B. Chizinga re-called, was when Ester discovered that one of their daughters was preg-nant.

Never in his life had he been as angry as when Ester told him the sad news. In his fury he demanded all the clothes from his daughter and immediately sent her away without any spare clothes. It was the white missionaries at Nkhoma, the Head mission station, who took her to live with them for a while until his wrath subsided after their pleading.

Among the three boys, Olafi, the youngest, was very scandalous and caused a lot of headache to his father. He was drinking and had no respect for other people's property. The last born was the first to die, shortly after his father's tragic death. The boy died a mysterious death and soon after his death, some people claimed responsibility. They claimed that his stealing habits were the cause for their retribution. He was buried next to his father's grave.

Kutchona had no favourite among the children. He treated them equally, including the adopted ones. One such child was Letison Kalambalala. He was brought into the family when he was only a toddler. Letison said about Kutchona's family, "it is wonderful how they brought me up. Everyone thought I was their real child. Every morning he would wake them up calling, "Time is money. If you lose ten minutes now, you will never recover them." Ikesi, however, recalls the words her father never forgot to recite when he came to wake her up, "We parents will not be with you forever. I do not want people to point fingers at my grave accusing me that I did not teach you household chores."

Naomi (Dorothy), Kutchona's daughter, one of the early graduates of Chancellor College

Apart from teaching his children household chores, Ikesi hails parents for forcing them to go to school and telling them to take school seriously. Most of Rev Kutchona's children, including the girls, went far enough with education and acquired employment. In the 1960s very few women were going to the University and Kutchona's daughter, Naomi, was one of the few cases. After she graduated from the University, she became a secondary school teacher. Alena is well employed with ADMARC, but Ikesi and Kaleni are now retired primary school teachers. This was a very rare achievement during Rev Kutchona's time.

Chapter 4

Hobbies and Preferences

Just like every person, Kutchona had personal preferences on drink, food and what to do with leisure time. Although he sometimes liked Fanta or Coke, tea was his number one beverage, which he took any time. Ikesi, making fun of her late father, said, "if he had his blood tested in the laboratory, the results would have revealed that tea formed more than 70% of his blood."

When it came to food, he was selective only when his pocket did not restrict him. Otherwise, when he had money he made sure he came home with a packet of rice and a chicken. If both *nsima* and rice lined up on the table with chicken as relish, he would put the *nsima* plate aside and drew the rice plate to himself—without break until the plate would be clean!

In dress, he loved to put on a white shirt, minding less about the colour of the trousers. Usually he walked without a tie on his neck. But when he was on duty he preferred the black shirt and dog collar to the white shirt, white tie, the uniform copied from the Dutch Reformed Church missionaries.

To change the subject: what did Kutchona like to do with his free time? He was an avid sucker of books; not only the bible and theological books, but secular books as well. Each night he read books until late, when everyone else had long gone to sleep. He also read during the day, when there were no visitors or church elders at home. Occasionally, he went to chat with friends, but he also liked to walk and travel and admire the wonderful creation of God.

Despite the conflict with the evangelist he had in Harare, Kutchona liked the scenery and landscape of Zimbabwe very much. Asking Dorothy what she thought would be the number one hobby of her late father, she promptly answered, "He loved travelling, seeing places and interesting geographical features." And quickly citing examples from Zimbabwe, "My late father traveled to see places of interest like Bulawayo, Umtali (Mutare) and others during the time we lived in Zimbabwe. He saw the greatness of God in the world which He had created." Dorothy also remembers how he went to the zoo by himself, and then came home excited and later organized to travel there with his whole family. It was the first time for Dorothy to see animals such as lions, leopards and crocodiles.

His quest for travel took him as far as the Indian Ocean. When he saw the ocean at Beira, he was overwhelmed by the vastness of the water mass. He was also amazed to see the huge ocean liners and cranes at the Beira port, comparing to nothing he had seen on Lake Malawi.

When he went back to his family, he ran short of words to describe what he had seen on that expedition. Filled with wonder, he just promised them that he would organize for them to travel to the ocean so that they would see those amazing things for themselves. But time went by and the visit to the ocean did not materialize. Everybody forgot about it, until the time for them to stay in Zimbabwe was up and it was time to go back to Nyasaland.

The train from Zimbabwe dropped them at Machipanda—a town in Mozambique—where they would change trains for the one to Malawi. It used to take some days. During that time the father told his wife and children to get ready for a journey to Beira.

Everyone was surprised, except Ester who whispered to them behind his back, "It has always been his dream. He never stopped talking to me

27

about it." Unfortunately, when they were about to start off for Beira, the port office announced the sad news that the time of departure for the Nyasaland train had been rescheduled. Early the following morning they would be going back home to Nyasaland.

On the train that took them to Nyasaland the outspoken Kutchona was conspicuously silent. He never took delight to look through the window at the speeding vegetation, mountains or rivers. Something about the abortive trip to Beira occupied his mind. Maybe he was seeing the tragic death he would meet at the birth of independence of his country, Malawi. It is possible he saw it in Limbo.

Chapter 5

Friends and Enemies

Before we look at the immediate circumstances surrounding his death, it must be mentioned that Reverend Alexander Kutchona would easily make enemies because of his provocative straightness and openness. Yet, because of the same reason, it was equally easy for him to attract people and make friends instantly.

Kutchona was a good storyteller. He loved to tell stories, mainly of the Ngoni expeditions and wars as they invaded Malawi through Mozambique. Mr S. Chikakuda remembers that people, even those that were not members of 'his' church, used to come to Kutchona's house in numbers, just to listen to his stories. He was a man of '*chikoka*,' who naturally drew people to himself.

Mr Tchete told me that Rev Kutchona had Asian friends too. In the early 1960s, there were three prominent Indian traders at Dedza Boma. One of them had acquired a Malawian name 'Chapalapata,' then there was Yusuf who owned "Highway Emporium" and "Randera." Kutchona was a friend to all of them and he used to go and chat with them mainly in the afternoon before sunset. All the three trusted him, for he used to take merchandise on credit.[11]

Among elders and parishioners, he had friends too. Mr. Chiwaula was one of his friends who tipped him with information at the time when enemies arose against him. Other intimate friends included a Mr. Jasten

---

[11]   B.J. Tchete, Nkhoma, June 2003.

and Mr Mzunga.[12] Rev Kutchona's daughters, Dorothy and Ikesi, remembered them well.

The late Reverend Ezara Mbewe and the then youthful outspoken preacher A.W.W. Mlenga Mbewe were some of his close friends among the clergy. Notice the clan name connection. Because of the clan name and resemblance in their outspokenness and lively preaching, Mlenga regarded him as his real father. He was the only clergy who sat at his death bed until he breathed his last.[13] Seemingly, Ezara was his brother. They both hailed from Dedza West and experienced similar assassination attempts. When these two Mbewes met, Ezara did much of the talking, sharing with his friend courageous encounters against enemy plots. Kutchona just laughed.

The two church ministers differed greatly in their preaching: Ezara preached long sermons that dragged a bit; Kutchona preached vivid and powerful sermons. They also differed significantly in their attitude towards enemies. Ezara had cleared all the hair on his head except his forehead, like the Zulu hero Chaka. But unlike Chaka he was very cautious with his enemies. He would not walk without a weapon of assault even for a short distance. But Kutchona had a spirit of "I do not care," sort of. Like Chaka, he was confident of himself and relaxed.

Some of Kutchona's intimate friends were among the Government's top brass in the district. Outstanding among them was a Mr Jack Chamanangwa, who was Officer in Charge, ADC, as it was known in those days. I could not establish whether he came from Chamangwana, a village at Katewe, adjacent to Kutchona's home. But the two used to visit each other in their homes very often. Jack reminds me of Joseph

---

12 Dorothy/Ikesi Kutchona, Richard Village, Maonde, Dedza, 5.4.2003.

13 Dorothy/Rev A.W.W. Mlenga, Nkhoma, June 2003.

of Arimathea or Nicodemus, who were friends of Jesus unto the grave, despite their stand in society.

Alexander had enemies too. Most of them were church members with good positions. Just as it was the case with Jesus, the man closest to him was the worst enemy. At Dedza CCAP station there was a man by the name of Makwangwala—popularly known as Khosi. He was a well-established evangelist in the church there. As such, he had a number of his loyalists among the church elders. His best friend among the elders was a Mr Gama. He was very influential too. The reason why the two people disliked Kutchona is still a mystery. It is possible that Khosi, as an established evangelist, enjoyed all the loyalty from church members before Kutchona came. And so, the minister's coming robbed him of the respect that he used to receive. Another possible cause is that the two, being Malawi Congress Party zealots, perceived Kutchona's messages as being anti-party and thought that he was a threat to the solidarity of the party.

With a cohort of Youth Leaguers, most of them members of the church, the two big fish joined hands with Mr Gomani, a business man at Dedza market, who held the formidable and notorious position of Head of the Youth League in the District, as Malanda and Tchete narrated.

Chapter 6

Circumstances Surrounding Kutchona's Death

From 1953, the year Kutchona left Mlanda for Harare, to December 1960, the time he came back to Nyasaland (Dedza congregation), the country had undergone tremendous political and social change. Hastings Kamuzu Banda had come in 1958 from England via Kumasi, Ghana. His open challenge to the white rule right from the day of his arrival and subsequent meetings—a thing no person in Malawi could ever dream to do—made him a hero and an idol among his people.[14]

A big fraction of the people aspiring to go into cabinet and parliament consisted of young educated people who had acquired ideologies and had passed them on to teachers even in the mission schools.[15] Christianity was questioned as the opium the whites were using in order to plunder and oppress the black race. According to my father, the late E.E. Katsulukuta, delegates to the highly politicized teachers' meeting for mission schools uttered sarcastic and insulting remarks against the church and her system and unanimously agreed to stop teaching Scripture in schools. All save my father and the late Chadza gave their consent to that decision.

Following Banda's arrest during the state of emergency in 1959 and his subsequent release from prison, the spirit of independence was kindled like flames of petrol fire. The zeal of the people was expressed by

---

[14] Martin Pauw, *Mission and Church in Malawi: the History of the Nkhoma Synod of the Church of Central Africa Presbyterian, 1889 – 1962*, Lusaka: BMP, pp. 123-124.

[15] Harry J. Kamwaza, *Senior Comprehensive History of Central Africa*, btq: Claim Blantyre, 2007, p. 127ff.

wearing party badges and buying party cards, both of which bore the face of Kamuzu the hero.

The Nyasaland African Congress[16] was not the sole party. The United Federal Party was next to MCP in popularity. Its members did not buy the MCP cards. And since it was a party accused of supporting white rule, its members were considered as traitors by the MCP cohorts, and traitors were given the name 'Kapilikoni.'[17] Since the badge and the party membership card were items to identify oneself with the MCP, a party for the indigenous people of Malawi and a symbol of unity, anyone without them was considered 'Kapilikoni.' Chief Kachere from Kutchona's home supported UFP and was a well-known 'Kapilikoni.'

The spirit of nationalism and the fight for independence had infiltrated into every sphere of life, including the church. Fanatics led by Khosi and Gama wanted to use the church as a forum to propagate party ideologies and launch a campaign against the whites. This was met with an immediate counter reaction from Kutchona. He forbade them to talk politics in the church, he even announced that no true Christian should wear a party badge in the church building. His sermons too were very direct; he meant to challenge Christians about their attitude of putting politics and Kamuzu above God. He also preached strongly against the malpractices of the Youth Leaguers, known as 'termites,' who used to harass people and sometimes cut down maize in the gardens of people who were suspected to be "traitors."

---

[16] Later to become the Malawi Congress Party.

[17] This comes from the Capricorn Africa Society, founded in 1949 by David Stirling and N.H. Wilson in Zimbabwe, which wanted a "partnership of Africans and immigrant Europeans working together ... for the benefit of both" (wiki Capricorn Africa Society).

Many people believe that Kutchona never bought a party card in his lifetime. They say for him buying a party card was an open act of worshipping the man. The District party office knew about this and they asked his adopted son Anderson, who had become the shadow MP for Dedza West, to persuade him to buy a party card. Anderson went to approach his uncle to persuade him to stop preaching against the party functionaries and also to accept party cards. But Rev Kutchona cut in before Anderson could finish. "I support Kamuzu myself, but you cannot force me to buy a card. Let people choose for themselves. And you cannot tell me to shut my mouth against the evils that your boys are inflicting on innocent people." So Anderson left.

In my investigations I found that the truth might actually be that Kutchona was indeed praying for Kamuzu and his party, and that he did even buy party cards. Long after he had died, his daughters were sorting out his books and they were surprised to find party cards from the earlier years when the cards were sold secretly.

Rev Y.A. Chienda, a younger contemporary of Kutchona, told me about a legend that circulated during that time: The Sunday following the day that Anderson met his stepfather, Kutchona went into the pulpit fully dressed as a Ngoni warrior, a shield in his left hand, a spear in his right hand, and a Bible and a hymn book under his armpit. "I cannot succumb to Anderson's threats", charged the man of God as he went into the pulpit. "Why should I follow the child play of Anderson?" However, it's a story that could not be substantiated.

The Youth League, a party wing for dealing with opposition and resistance, labeled Kutchona as number one Kapilikoni. Every Sunday they came to Dedza CCAP Church in their red shirts and khaki trousers with black stripes on the sides. They came with clubs, sticks and panga knives, which they left at the doorstep as they entered the church building. It must be noted that these individuals who disliked Kutchona were hiding behind the party. Their acts were not in accordance with the party's constitution, though the party covered them up.

There is another story, which says that when Kutchona was in the pulpit one Sunday, a certain gentleman, wearing a party badge on the flap of his jacket, came into the church with a loud tapping of laced shoes. He walked all the way to sit in the front seat. The preacher stopped talking to gaze at the man until he was about to sit. Then he commanded him, "Don't sit. If you want to sit in this church, take off that badge on your jacket. If you can't you should just walk out." And the man chose to march out. "We come into this building because we are children of God and we seek to see the face of our Father God. Why should someone wear a face of a person to disrupt our attention from God our Father. You are free, Monday to Saturday, to put that face on your jackets. Put that badge on when you go to party meetings." Addressing the congregation, he concluded, "we gather in this building to seek audience with God our Father."

The Sunday that followed this incident, Kutchona was surprised that Khosi and Gama were missing in the vestry session before the service. But when he entered into the main church, he noted that there were many more red shirts than usual. He could not guess what the Youth Leaguers intended to do on that particular Sunday. Gama and Makwangwala, also wearing Youth League uniforms, were seated in the parlour.

But when the church minister stood up and greeted the congregation to start the service, Khosi and Gama rose and ordered him to step down or else the congregation would march out. "Everybody march out" they charged when they saw that Kutchona did not comply. "We cannot attend a service led by a useless Kapilikoni."

All the congregants remained seated because they did not know what to do. When the Youth Leaguers saw that the congregants remained seated, they all stood up with sticks in their hands and threatened to use force if the people would remain seated. Thus everyone hurried out in fear. And when the church was empty, Kutchona was the last to walk out through the vestry door to the manse that was fifty yards away. An emergency church council was called the same week and it was agreed that Makwangwala and Gama be disciplined. From that day on the two became raving wolves openly swearing to cut Kutchona's throat.[18]

As opposition intensified, Kutchona's preaching became more soul touching than ever before. In his preaching he emphasized the futility of earthly life as compared to the reliability of the heavenly life. The impact of his sermons was felt in the neighbouring Mlanda congregation. The minister there was Reverend Chimombo, a fanatic member of the Malawi Congress Party. He wore the badge with the head of Kamuzu even on his preaching gown, on the pulpit and during funeral services.

Chimombo began to preach counter messages that were somehow heretic. He said Kamuzu was the Messiah of the time designated by God. So any person who despises the wearing of party badges is against God's authority and will not enter heaven. The Synod was alarmed by his dangerous teachings and they sent envoys to caution him, but Chimombo was arrogant to them as well. Hence the Synod ruled that Chimombo be excommunicated and he was ordered to leave Mlanda. Mlanda being a Ngoni dominated congregation, the Synod assigned a Ngoni minister, Reverend Ezara Mbewe, to replace him.[19]

---

[18] S.E. Chikakuda, Dedza, 5.5.2003.

[19] Rev K.J. Mgawi, Chongoni, 6.5.2003.

On 6th July 1964 Dr Hastings Kamuzu Banda and his Malawi Congress Party won the elections and the country received its Independence. During that time the plot to kill Kutchona was an open secret in Dedza Township. Rev Kutchona and his family heard the rumours. Sometimes people passing by would shout these threats loud enough for them to hear, especially in the evening.[20] Anderson came again to warn his stepfather and advise him to ask for a transfer, but he refused. It is not known where these party people held their meetings, but they asked Anderson whether he had been successful in forcing his father to repent or not. Anderson replied, "Ndalephera" (I have failed). With these words Rev Kutchona, the man of God, was betrayed.[21]

The first serious attempt by his enemies to kill him was made one night when Kutchona was just beginning to sleep. In his half sleep, he thought he had heard a heavy knock at the front door; and he raised his head. His wife stopped him, "Where are you going?" she whispered. But before he could answer, there came another heavy knock. Ignoring his wife he sprang out of bed and rushed to the sitting room. "Who are you?" he was trying to sound undisturbed. The man knocking outside did not say who he was. Instead he told a story of a friend of Kutchona from Zimbabwe who was in transit. The bus on which he was travelling had a breakdown at Dedza Bus Stage. The bus was being repaired. The friend would very much like to meet him. Unfortunately he could not carry his luggage with him because it was too big. Besides he was afraid that he would miss the bus should it get repaired while he was away.

Though the pastor knew that the night caller was not alone and that they had come to kill him, he did not sound suspicious. He replied, "I

[20] Dorothy and Ikesi Kutchona, Richard Village, Maonde, Dedza, 5.4.2003; S.E. Chikakuda, Dedza, 5.5.2003.

[21] B.J. Tchete, Nkhoma, June 2003.

am sorry that I cannot go to see him, because I am suffering from malaria since evening. But go and bring him with you. If the night bus leaves him, he will sleep here and take the morning bus."

As the caller was leaving, he peeped through the window. He saw a number of people joining him from behind the church building. He took his spear and his shield and he kept on watching them from the window as they were killing time to deceive him and make him think that the night caller had really gone to call the visitor from Zimbabwe at the bus stage.

When the people called again, he quickly opened the door, raised a war alarm whistle from his lips as he danced round and round with his weapons of war in both hands. It was a war dance challenging them to come forward. Then he charged towards them dispersing them as each ran for his life. He came back to his house and did not sleep until morning.

This incident was the first attempt by his enemies to take his life. He reported it to the church council and the elders advised him that he should never come out of the house during the night. However, the session decided to excommunicate Khosi and Gama.

The Synod is rumoured to have sent two people to plead with him to accept a posting to another congregation.[22] As the two envoys broke the news, the man of God fell on his knees and prayed, "God please forbid! I cannot run away from death. I do not preach a gospel of my own. If I move from Dedza, what other gospel is there for me that I can preach?"[23]

---

[22] I could not confirm this.

[23] Rev B.L. Chizinga, Mtakataka Dedza, 1998.

However, this rumour may have arisen from a visit of two big men of the Synod, the Moderator and the General Secretary, as they were coming from Mlanda where there had been a bloody collision between the opposing factions of Chimombo and Ezara Mbewe. Though the Synod had ordered Chimombo to leave Mlanda and had sent Rev Ezara Mbewe to replace him, Chimombo had refused to leave Mlanda and about half of the congregation supported him; and they continued to hold services in the church building, while Rev Ezara Mbewe held services with the remaining half under a tree outside the church building. The two factions were like cat and dog. Being Ngoni warriors, both factions went to church with shields and spears. And it happened one Sunday morning, after exchanging bitter words, that the two groups engaged in a bloody fight. At least one person died, though the government did all it could to conceal this sad development for obvious reasons.

Rev Mwale and Rev Mgawi had gone to Mlanda to resolve the conflict and Rev Chimombo was ordered to leave Mlanda with immediate effect. When the two emissaries called at Dedza as they came back from Mlanda, they decided to share this with Kutchona, who would be interested to know about these sad developments at Mlanda, a church where he had previously served and which was also a neighbouring congregation.

As the VW Beetle in which the envoys had come started off, he lifted his hand and waved them goodbye. He stood there until the tail of the car disappeared. He would not see them again. Time was ticking down fast for him. In a week's time he too would disappear; disappear into the debris of the independence eruptions that were at that time shaking Africa and Malawi in particular.

Chapter 7

The Brutality of the Independence Eruption

Dedza CCAP congregation, as they solemnly walked out of the church the Sunday that followed Rev Mwale's visit, admitted that they had never heard Kutchona preach as movingly as he did on that particular Sunday. It was his last Sunday sermon. On the following Wednesday he was brutally beaten which led to his untimely death.

After the Wednesday afternoon prayer session which took place between three and four he said to his wife: "Mother, I go to Randera to get breakfast for tomorrow." Looking at the table watch and gauging the sun, she thought there was still ample time before it would become dark. "Surely, it's not too late," she thought.

They did not know that the people who were looking for his life had placed out sentinels day and night. As soon as they saw him heading for the trading centre through his usual shortcut behind the Wenela offices, the sentries ran to the people who had plotted for his life. As he entered Yusufu's shop and then Randera's, the plotters were taking positions behind banana trees in the bush. Some stood behind the blue gum trees that stretched from the Wenela Building to the Trading Centre.

Some people gave him a quick, pitiful glance as he came out of Randera's shop, because they knew what he would meet in a few minutes to come. Other eyes were deliberately avoiding him. The impending ambush was not a secret at the trading centre, because the plotters had openly boasted about it. Yet no one told Rev Kutchona about the plot.

A loaf of bread in his left and two packets of sugar in his right hand, his homeward step was quick. Tall blue gum trees lined both sides of the path for a distance. Ahead of the blue gum there were *sanga* trees. One of them was stunted in growth and it stood right next to the shortcut path. He looked back before he entered the bushy path. Behind him a girl was following at a distance. She was not one of his flock, but she knew him well.

Suddenly, appearing from the bushes, strong young men encircled him with sticks, clubs and panga knives. All were familiar faces. One of them was a messenger at the District Commissioner's office, he came from Ntcheu, and another one was a messenger at the council and he hailed from Mangochi. Some of them were members of his church. He charged, "What do you want?" he showed no fear.

But his adversaries were not in the mood to converse with him. One of the messengers aimed a club at his forehead. But it landed on his intercepting crossed arms. Then a range of weaponry rained down on him. As he was protecting his head with his right hand, it was totally crushed. The girl who was coming behind him stopped, startled. She saw him falling on his knees, begging one more favour from his killers. "Give me one moment to pray to my God." This request was answered by a club on his head and a panga at the back of his head. He was flattened, prostrated across the path. They continued to beat him and probably thought that he was dead. The girl began to run through the bush by another path that led to her home. The picture of a man of God kneeling and asking his killers to allow him to pray was a haunt that always revamped to bless and encourage her. She shared this experience with Dorothy many years later.

Meanwhile his wife, Ester, and the children were panicking at home. "Father ought to have come by now," she thought and paced to and fro in the house. She even went out to look in the direction he ought to have come from, but there was no sign of him.

However, Kutchona revived, though he never regained full consciousness. There are two stories that explain how he got back home. The most popular one says that when the cool evening breeze (*mwera*) blew over him, he came back to life and crawled slowly until he reached home. He began calling his wife as he struggled to get up the steps. His wife heard a call, but it was too ghostly to be recognized, until the children forced her to open; and there he was, blood oozing freely from nose, ears and mouth.[24]

Chikakuda, his cousin and R. Malanda, working at Wenela at that time, have a different version. They were in their office at about four o'clock when some people reported to him that Kutchona had been beaten severely. He and several church elders went to the scene. Kutchona was still breathing. The elders improvised a stretcher from wood and the bark of the trees. They picked him up on the stretcher.[25]

He was definitely only semi-conscious. Ester in total surprise exclaimed: "What is it, father!" He recognized her voice. He tried to answer her, but all he could say was: "I am not alright."

Ester was wiping blood from his nose, ears, mouth and the back of his head as he lay groaning on his bed. However, she remembered to send a message to Ikesi who was staying with her husband at the DC's quarters. When Ikesi talked to her father he gave the same answer, "I am not alright." Blood continued to ooze from the wounds, and Ester was wiping it away with her *chitenje*, which soon got soaked.

Some of his children went to report to the police. Since the officer-in-charge was a personal friend to Kutchona, they expected the police to act with a sense of urgency. But they were disappointed over their

---

[24] This version is shared even by his daughters, Ikesi and Dorothy.

[25] Mr. Malanda, working for Wenela at that time, also confirmed this.

reception there. They definitely did not treat the case with the urgency it deserved. The police never asked questions, they never visited the scene and they did not open a file for the case, as it was characteristic of the police at that time.

However, as a friend, Chamangwana did come to see Kutchona as the latter lay groaning in his bed. And Kutchona told him too: "I am not alright."

Chamangwana had come in a police car. A few minutes later Anderson Kutchona (MP) came driving in his car. Ester's prayers had been answered. It cannot be recalled which one of the two vehicles took Kutchona to Dedza Hospital. And it was a relief when he was referred from Dedza Hospital to Lilongwe District Hospital, popularly known as the Bottom Hospital. Ester and Dorothy went along to look after him. Rev A.W.W. Mlenga was minister of Lilongwe CCAP at the time and frequented Kutchona's deathbed with words of comfort and lots of prayers. He phoned the Synod office at Nkhoma.

The news of the tragic incident spread like wildfire. Rev B.K. Chizinga heard about it as he was travelling by bus from Kasinje to Nkhoma. Two women were conversing in riddles as the bus pulled up at Dedza bus stage. "Have you heard the news about the CCAP minister of this congregation. He is badly injured," one of them started. "Injured by what?" enquired the other. "A pawpaw tree fell on him. Figure it out for yourself." Chizinga could not make head or tail of the conversion. He disembarked at Kamphata, hoping to take a lift to Nkhoma where he intended to meet the General Secretary.

Barely a minute after Chizinga had arrived at Kamphata, the General Secretary's car came from Nkhoma heading for Lilongwe. He ran and waved to stop it. "It is good that I have met you," said the General Secretary as he opened the door to greet Chizinga. I am rushing to

Lilongwe hospital to visit Kutchona now battling for his life after party cohorts beat him brutally. Now do me one favour. As I go to see him, please go to Dedza and console the family on my behalf."

Rev K.J. Mgawi, the General Secretary, was the last person Kutchona talked to. When he had given his usual reply, "I am not alright," he began to gasp for air. He gasped throughout Thursday night and he breathed his last around 10.00 am on Friday.[26] His body was taken to his home at Katewe, Richard village, Chikoma, in Dedza West area for his burial.

---

[26] Mrs Cilembwe (nee Dorothy Kutchona), Falls Estate Lilongwe, October 2002, 5.4.2003.

Chapter 8

Buried in the Debris of the Independence Eruption

The 17th of December 1964, the possible day that Kutchona was buried, was a rainy day. All roads went to Katewe on that day. Though the soil texture was sticky clay, cars still risked to travel on muddy roads. Among the swerving cars was a seven tonner from Dedza congregation. And the Women's Guild was singing the popular song of that time.[27]

> One: Velonica
>
> All: Velonica'we
>
> One: Velonica
>
> All: Velonica'we
>
> Velonica, mwana wa mwini wamtani - Velonica'we

Despite the downpour, this funeral attracted a lot of people. The clergy included Reverends Mwale, Mgawi, Kamphinda, Mlenga, Y.A. Chienda, Chizinga, just to mention a few, and South African missionaries A.C. Human and C.J. Burger.

Honourable Anderson Kutchona Mbewe was notably present. Mr Malanda remembers that relatives asked him not to attend the funeral and he left. However, the people's attention was focused on Mr Chamangwana, the officer in charge of Dedza Police. He was representing Government at this funeral. When time came for him to speak on behalf of the Government, the people stretched their ears to catch every word he would say. It is not surprising that people still

---

27 Rev Khulungira Masina, Nkhoma, Lilongwe, Sept 2003.

remember what he said, though they can't mention the theme of the sermon of that day.

People noted how Chamangwana was carefully selecting a lot of vague words. "When I came to see him on his bed, I observed that something had been done ... As a professional policeman I very much wished I could bring to book all the culprits..." and in a gesture of despair he concluded: "...but you know how things are nowadays..."

When Chamangwana finished talking, Rev J.S. Mwale preached a powerful sermon. But nobody remembers the Scripture reading. All that people recall is that he consoled the bereaved and assured believers of victory in Jesus Christ.

That is how the late Kutchona's body was buried. It was symbolic of hundreds of people (including many Jehovah's Witnesses) who died brutally at the hands of Youth Leaguers, falsely accusing them of being traitors of the movement for independence.[28] His unattended tomb represents many tombs from Karonga to Nsanje which were not even known by their relatives; their own people could not even ask about them for fear of being accused of being disloyal to Kamuzu and the party.

Barely a week after this tragic burial of a man of God, Rev Killion Mgawi, the General Secretary, wrote a letter to Dedza Police on behalf of the Synod demanding that the police give a statement on the death

---

[28] For the persecution of the Jehovah's Witnesses see: Klaus Fiedler, "Power at the Receiving End: The Jehovah's Witnesses' Experience in One Party Malawi," in Kenneth R. Ross (ed), *God, People and Power in Malawi: Democratization in Theological Perspective*, Blantyre: CLAIM-Kachere, 1996, pp. 149-176; repr. in Klaus Fiedler, *Conflicted Power in Malawian Christianity: Essays Missionary and Evangelical from Malawi*, Mzuzu: Mzuni Press, 2015, pp. 112-142, - For persecutions immediately before and after independence see pp. 117-118.

of one of their clergy. The police replied vaguely to this enquiry. The reply letter said the Police has been instructed not to say anything on Kutchona's death. So Kutchona's burial also signified the many graves and mysterious cases that had been craftily buried so that no one would dare exhume them for a postmortem. There is no record of Kutchona's death, not even in the Archives where the records and the correspondence of the Synod are kept. (The mysterious disappearance of revealing documents was not strange.)

Hopefully, the devil has not tampered with the records in heaven as well. When the books will be opened, maybe then we will know exactly what happened.

Chapter 9

Divine Vengeance

When people were gathered at Dedza CCAP Church for transport arrangements to Kutchona's home, Katewe, there came a man— Kutchona's friend from Ntcheu. He was a pastor of the Seventh-day Adventist Church at Lakeview. He carried a bag at his back and he came hurriedly. Unceremoniously, but prophetically he addressed the crowd through prayer, saying, "God, my heavenly Father, you've promised that it is your duty to revenge. The innocent blood of your faithful servant has been shed. Will you not vindicate the life of your servant...?"[29]

From the day that Kutchona was beaten, three people who were members of the Youth League and messengers in government departments, had frequent hallucinations and they showed signs of being half-insane. They would wake up at night naked and walk in the streets of Dedza as if they were going to work. It did not take time before Anderson became inflicted by the same illness. He too would walk by night and forget to put on his clothes as he went to the DC's office. In addition to the mental illness, he developed wounds on his skin two years after Kutchona's death. It seems it was skin cancer and it did not respond to medical treatment. The hair on his head fell out and his skin was wrinkled and lost appearance. His cousin Matonga, who was working with the Ministry of Agriculture at Madisi or Ntchisi, took him to try out some traditional healers. He died while at a traditional healer and he was buried without proper ceremony.

---

[29] S.E. Chikakuda, Dedza, 5.5.2003. Both Chikakuda and Tchete remembered this episode well.

God's revenging hand did not leave one of those who lifted a hand to kill Kutchona; they all died with different ailments. So God Himself did what the police could not do!

Bibliography

Daneel, Inus, *Mbiri ya CCAP Harare Sinodi 1912-1982*, Harare: CCAP Synod, 1982.

Kamwana, Jonathan, "The Spirituality of Rev. J.S. Mwale," DTh, Stellenbosch University, 1997.

Kamwaza, Harry, *Senior Comprehensive History of Central Africa*, Blantyre: CLAIM, 2007.

Labuschagne, A.S., *The Missionary*, Fichardtpark: Drufoma Press, 2000.

Pauw, Martin, *Mission and Church in Malawi: the History of the Nkhoma Synod of the Church of Central Africa, Presbyterian 1889-1962*, Wellington: CLF, 2016.

Ross, Kenneth R. and Klaus Fiedler, *A Malawi Church History 1860 – 2020*, Mzuzu: Mzuni Press, 2020, esp. chapters 10 and 14.

Interviews

Banda, Rev S.S., Mvera, 2004.

Chienda, Rev Y.A., Chongoni, Dedza, 5.5.2003.

Chikakuda, S.E., Dedza, 5.5.2003.

Cilembwe, Mrs (nee Dorothy Kutchona), Falls Estate Lilongwe, October 2002, 5.4.2003.

Chinkhadze, Rev M.Z., Lumbadzi, Lilongwe, 17.2.2003.

Chizinga, Rev B.L., Mtakataka, Dedza, 1998.

Kalambalala, Letison, Richard Village Maonde, Dedza, 5.4.2003.

Kambirinya, E.G., Kamvuwu, Dowa, 22.4.2003.

Kutchona, Ikesi, Richard Village, Maonde, Dedza, 5.4.2003.

Malanda, R.C.A., Kawale, Lilongwe, June 2004.

Mgawi, Rev K.J., Chongoni, 6.5.2003.

Masina, Rev H.J.C, Nkhoma, Lilongwe, June 2004.

Mlenga, Rev A.W.W, Nkhoma, June 2003.

Tchete, B.J., Nkhoma, June 2003.

Printed in the United States
By Bookmasters